Bideford Bay to Torrington

12 Rural and Coastal Walks

by
Tony Chapman

By the same author:

Walking to Good Purpose   (1) The Parish Churches of Exmoor
                                    (2) Around South Molton
                                      (3) Barnstaple (North and East)
                                      (4) Barnstaple (South and West

ISBN 0 9535321 8 6

A CIP catalogue record for this book is obtainable from the British Library

Printed by
Avocet Press, Cullompton, Devon

Published by
R.M Young, 17 Broad Street, South Molton, Devon EX36 3AQ

The moral rights of the author have been asserted.

All photographs are the copyright of the author.

Cover photograph: The bridge and weir at Beam

INDEX OF WALKS

Walk Number	Route	Page
1	Appledore-Coast Path-Northam-Cleve	10
2	Westward Ho!-Coast Path-Abbotsham-Lake	16
3	Ford-Alwington-Horns Cross-Peppercombe-Coast Path-Cockington	22
4	Littleham-Summerhill-W.Ashridge	28
5	Littleham-Woodtown-Buckland Brewer-Rudha	32
6	Buckland Brewer-Newhaven-Parkham-Babeleigh	38
7	Monkleigh-Saltrens-Looseham-Buckland Brewer-Higher Culleigh	44
8	Weare Gifford-Gammaton Moor-East-the-Water-Tarka Trail (S)-Annery	50
9	Weare Gifford-Huntshaw Mill-Gammaton Moor-Hallspill	58
10	Torrington-Norwood Bridge-Huntshaw Mill-Weare Gifford-Tarka Trail (S)	62
11	Torrington-Tarka Trail (N)- Monkleigh-Frithelstock-Watergate-Tarka Trail (N)	68
12	Torrington-TarkaTrail (S)-Watergate-Southcott-Langtree-Taddiport	74

Watering Holes

Walk

1   **Spoilt for Choice**

2   **Abbotsham** — The Thatched Inn

3   **Horns Cross** — Coach & Horses

4/5   **Littleham** — Crealock Arms

5/6   **Buckland Brewer** — Coach & Horses

6   **Parkham** — The Bell Inn

7   **Monkleigh** — The Bell Inn

8/9   **Weare Gifford** — Cyder Presse

10   **Torrington** — Many & Various
           Weare Gifford — Cyder Presse

11   **Torrington** — Puffing Billy
           Monkleigh — The Bell Inn
           Frithelstock — Clinton Arms

12   **Torrington** — Puffing Billy
           Langtree — The Green Dragon

Places on Route

Name	Walk No.
Abbotsham	2
Alwington	3
Appledore	1
Babeleigh	6
Beam	11
Bocombe	6
Buckland Brewer	5-6-7
Burrough	5-7
Cleve (Bideford)	1
East-the-Water	8
Fairoak	9
Fairy Cross	3
Ford	3
Foxdown	6
Frithelstock	11
Frithelstockstone	12
Goldworthy	3
Hallspill	9

Name	Walk No.
Horns Cross	3
Lake	2
Langtree	12
Littleham	4-5
Looseham	5-7
Monkleigh	7-11
Newhaven	6
Northam	1
Parkham	6
Saltrens	7
Southcott	12
Taddiport	12
Thorne	5-7
Torrington	10-11-12
Watergate	11-12
Weare Gifford	8-9-10
Westward Ho!	2
Woodtown	3-5

PRE-RAMBLE

Walking as a pastime is becoming increasingly popular nowadays and few pleasurable pursuits can be more rewarding from a health point of view. One of the developments in this field of activity has been the big increase in guided walks centred on tourist "honeypots" with the emphasis on popular, established trails like the Tarka Trail. While this approach to walking for pleasure obviously offers a useful service for the occasional outing or family groups on holiday the slightly more serious walker will be looking for something else. Many will prefer to explore the more remote by-ways at their own pace and in their own time.

In this particular area The Tarka Trail; South West Coast Path, Two Moors Way etc. are all glorious walks ideal for the serious walker but this book sets out to provide for those who just enjoy exploring the countryside without being too serious about it. However, these attractions have not been entirely ignored. The various walks include over ten miles of the coast path from Northam to Peppercombe and the Tarka Trail from East-the-Water to Watergate Bridge, some seven miles.

North Devon has a remarkable variety of beautiful moor land and some of the finest sandy beaches in the country. It is not surprising therefore that the tourists' interests are directed towards these impressive amenities in a way which tends to detract from the equally delightful countryside inland. The walks in this book seek to redress the balance in one area of North Devon, namely, from Appledore on the coast to south of Torrington.

Much of the walking is along quiet country roads and lanes which makes it suitable for most weather conditions. The format is designed for the convenience of walkers who are quite happy to drive a few miles, park the car and do a circular walk. As all the walks are based on a village there is always a church to visit for anyone who appreciates these ancient treasures. Just to mention one particularly splendid example, a visit to the Parish Church at Alwington (walk 3 and 5) is certainly recommended. Perhaps reference should also be made (in the interest of impartiality) to the fact that being village based there is at least one watering hole to be found on each walk although this is of course purely coincidental.

Most of the walks in the book are on two OS Maps, namely, EXPLORER 126 and 139. The walks 1 and 2 appear only on Map 139 and the most southerly four (walks 9 to 12) only on map 126. The remainder are common to both. The map required is indicated at the head of each individual walk.

It might be appropriate to add a note on the folding of maps for the benefit of the uninitiated. The OS Maps are pre-folded to form a compact, manageable pack but once open it is as if the genie is out of the bottle and seemingly unwilling to get back in to it. There is one way and one way only to re-pack it and that is correctly because any other way can cause awful confusion with damage to the map (and to one's reputation if force and profanity are practiced). Add a strong wind and cold hands and all the elements for a comedian's hilarious sketch are present. For anyone not familiar with these maps it is advisable to work it all out in comfort of the living room! Apart from any other consideration maps are quite expensive to replace.

Do not endeavour to economise by saving on the cost of an Ordnance map. Without a map it is easy to become irretrievably lost - an embarrassment devoutly to be missed! However detailed the text it is possible to make the occasional navigational error and without the benefit of a map the stranger to the area is at a big disadvantage. Apart from any other consideration an OS Map really does "talk" to you about the countryside in the areas around you.

On private land keep to the public right of way without straying on to adjacent land. A possible exception to this is where a public footpath is routed across an arable field when the considerate walker may well prefer to go round the edge rather than trample growing crops. Some farmers are their own worst enemy where walkers are concerned. If there is an established right of way over their property it is in all our interests that the route is kept free of obstruction and clearly marked. We must remember that in rural areas maps are revised and brought up to date very infrequently and the lay-out of farms can change significantly over the years in which case it is even more desirable for the route to be way marked properly. Where it is difficult to reconcile the line shown on the map with what you see on the ground be patient and endeavour to refrain from causing avoidable damage to farm property. After all a country walk is meant to relax us-not to raise our blood pressure (or the farmer's!).

A few words on the subject of road drill may be appropriate for anyone new to this kind of walking. The general rule is to keep to the right hand side of the road to face oncoming traffic but like all rules there are exceptions. Where there is no verge on the right and there is one on the other side then it is clearly safer to use it. On sharp right hand bends great care is needed and often it is safer to use the left-hand side of the road, which allows motorists a little more time to see you. Human flesh versus flying metal is an uneven contest so take care at all times.

A further useful thing to bear in mind on very narrow lanes particularly when there is a strong wind into your face is to keep the ears attuned to the noise of vehicles approaching from behind. Stand well aside, mingling with the hedge if necessary, but make quite sure you look back to see there is nothing else coming before moving out again. On country lanes it is not unusual for cars to come along like the proverbial buses - two or three at a time.

One final point. The walks described in this book are as they were at the time of walking them and the situation on the ground may well vary under different weather conditions and the time of year.

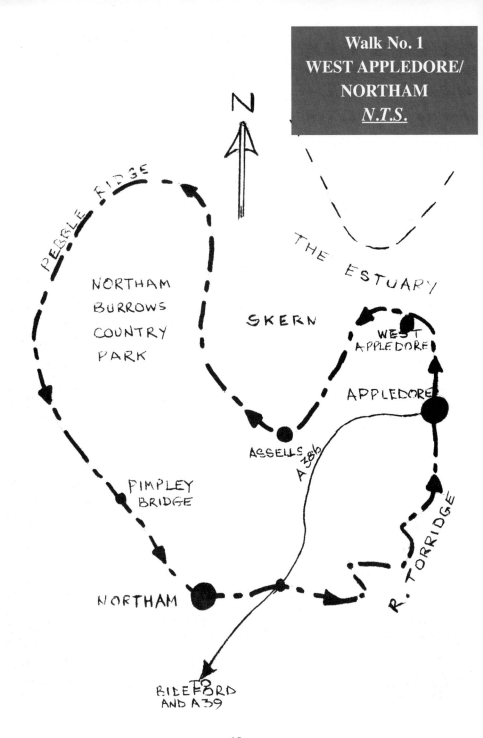

Walk No.1 WEST APPLEDORE/NORTHAM

West Appledore — SW Coast Path — Sandymere — Pimpley Bridge— Northam –The Cleve — West Appledore.

8 miles. *Map — OS Explorer 139.*

Parking : Use the large public car park at West Appledore.

Appledore is off the main tourist routes, which is greatly to its advantage as far as the discerning visitor is concerned. It is one of those peaceful waterside places, which are fast disappearing in this commercialised age. There is a rich history to explore together with sufficient modern amenities to satisfy present needs. For the walker planning to do the walk it would be advisable to allow plenty of time before setting out (or at the end) just to savour the delights of this fascinating resort.

Having parked the car and paid the appropriate fee (£1:40 a day in 2002) get on to the road in front of the Church. The road is actually on the route of the SW coast path, which we will be following for just over a mile. Turn right to go into the narrow but intriguing Irsha Street with its little cluster of houses off each side. Note t he rich variety of house names many of

The Taw/Torridge Estuary

which give a clue to the maritime history of Appledore. The area exudes a feeling of history, one name alone "Fish Stories Spoken Here", tells it all.

However, keep moving to pass the Beaver Inn (fresh fish on the menu here!) and the Royal George. At the end of Irsha Street be prepared for a stunning view of Bideford Bar (no connection with the aforesaid hostelries), with Crow point on the far side of the estuary and out across the Skern to Grey Sand Hill. Across the notorious Bar countless generations of fishermen have put to sea on their hazardous occupation including the men who sailed from here in 1588 to fight the Spanish Armada.

Follow the road down past the old Custom House and more modern Lifeboat station before going up some steps on to the narrow path along the top of the bank. This is the real coast path and is well signed along here. Take care because the path is really narrow and a little rough underfoot with quite a severe drop on the seaward side.

After a while the brambles and nettles give way to a pleasant walk over fields to a point which marks the parting of the ways, again well signed. A ladder leads down on to the beach to allow walkers to go along the foreshore at times of low water. This route is obviously unmistakable so we will use the inshore walk, which is itself quite straightforward. Carry on past the steps to join the road at Watertown Garage and then straight along Long Lane with a somewhat unusual "rush" hedge on the right hand side.

At the crossroads turn right for a short distance with a large sign proclaiming entry to the Northam Burrows Country Park facing you at which point the low and high water routes meet up again. Turn left to cross Appledore Bridge and pause to read and digest the wording of a huge notice setting out a whole schedule of what visitors must not do, including speeds in excess of 20 mph (so just watch it!). The coast path takes the line of the road although it is far more pleasant to walk along the grass, which presumably is permissible since it is not listed on the sign as being verboten.

You are now in a wide expanse of burrows with the water (or mud/sand) of the Skern according to tidal conditions on the right. Keep going along the road which bears around to the right towards Grey Sand Hill and which ends at the car park outside, of all things, a recycling collection depot. Environmentalists and recycling zealots with a particular penchant for these things may well find the site so fascinating they will proceed no further but is only mentioned here as a point of reference on the walk. Moves are afoot apparently to abandon the site if a suitable alternative can be found in a less sensitive area but it seems no one wants to live in the vicinity of so desirable an amenity.

Leaving the controversial site astern we take the path towards the estuary, which is reached after passing the neck of Grey Sand Hill. For those of us unable to walk on water it is necessary to turn left at this point to proceed on a route parallel to the waters edge. There is in fact what appears to be a flood bank along the first part which make for some pleasant walking and which could be an advantage in very wet conditions.

On reaching the northern extremity of the burrows a closer view of the notorious Bideford Bar comes into view. The Bar is dangerous on account of the shallowness and fierce tidal rips which only an experienced mariner should attempt to cross. Along this stretch there are several notices warning people not to venture into the water — advice which should never be disregarded.

A little further along be prepared to meet a hazard facing all who walk in the area, namely a man-made phenomenon in the form of a golf links — the Royal North Devon Golf Course no less, the oldest course in England. Since it has been used for over a century any scars as a result of injury received in passing through maybe worn with pride. Just beware of flying, unguided missiles. Little round things, they are generally white, sometimes yellow and very occasionally red but whatever the colour the result of personal contact is much about the same. Should you hear a frantic call of FORE! bellowed in your direction dive for cover if there is any, otherwise just dive.

In between taking avoiding action against random mishits proceed along the path inshore of the dunes and keep close to the fence. Although you will probably come face to face with a party of golfers bear in mind that the general public have right of way at all times and all players are aware of and respect this. Eventually the Golf Course is left behind for the time being and the path ends at a huge sandy car park with the Burrows Centre building on the left as you reach it.

The car park area is a very good place to pause for a snack (and somewhat safer than the 7th fairway), to admire the pebble ridge, which protects the Burrows from being flooded by the sea, and to listen to the sound of the waves coming ashore with the screeches of seagulls wheeling overhead. From the car park leave the coast path and turn inland at the Y junction onto the roadway with the tower of Northam Church on the skyline ahead. Again keep a watchful eye for flying golf balls because this road actually runs through the course.

All danger from errant golfers is over once Pimpley Bridge is reached and we return to the built-up area of Northam. Pass the Sandymere Sports Centre and keep straight on for the town centre where it is well worthwhile to climb the steps on the right both to take in the sea views and also to have a look around the historic St Margaret's, the Parish Church of Northam. An unusually detailed and interesting guide by a Mr Gale is on sale inside. Northam itself, like Appledore, has a rich history and great charm but does of course lack the intimate seaside atmosphere of the latter.

Once in the square turn off along North Street past the Post Office and bear right at the end where it meets the main road into Appledore. Carry on down the road to the left towards Appledore as far as Bloody Corner. This is the place where in the year 892 the Danish King Hubba was slain by our own King Harold. Nowadays there is probably as much danger of being killed as a pedestrian trying to cross the road. The name Bloody Corner derives from the battle of course and not from any observation by a scuttling walker. Either way take good care in the crossing because it is dangerous.

Immediately opposite there is the memorial stone commemorating the battle at which point a private road begins. There is a public right of way along this road which allows some fine views of the river and with some very old but still splendid fir trees on one side.

Re-join the coastal path at the signpost by climbing the stile on the left and begin a short walk through what is quite a rural oasis set amid extensive urban development. Be careful not to miss the right turn over a stream at the bottom of this field (it is signposted). Go straight down over the field and keeping a sharp look-out for a well - concealed stile in the fence on the left. A short length of footpath leads past the crowning glory of present-day Appledore - the largest entirely covered shipyard in Europe. Shipbuilding continues to prosper in this historic area in which replicas of Drake's "Golden Hind" and the "Nonsuch" have been built here in recent times. However, some fine modern ships continue to be built including the latest survey ship for the Admiralty, which was launched recently.

Turn left on to a narrow lane at the T-junction but not for long. A footpath turns off on the right-hand side through something of a wilderness and which leads to a road where we turn right to pass through the industrial past of Appledore including the main entrance to the covered shipyard. This is an area that few tourists will see but it does have some interesting characteristics both ancient and modern.

The welcoming sign of "The Bell Inn" confirms you are back in the comfort zone of Appledore. Just along the road the vast gantry rotting away in the old Richmond Dock is a last glimpse of its history and where the road from the shipyard meets the main road turn right to enjoy a superb walk along the Marine Parade. Thus ends a delightful 8 mile walk through a very interesting variety of environments.

Appledore Shipyard

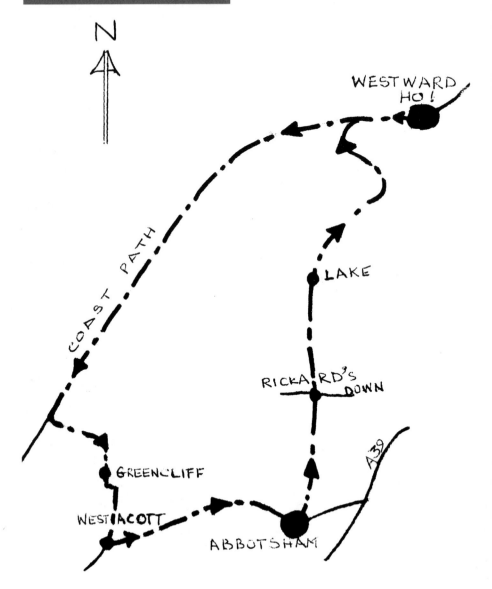

WALK NO.2 WESTWARD WO!/ABBOTSHAM

Westward Ho! — Rock Nose — Cornborough & Abbotsham Cliffs (The SW Coast Path) — Greencliff — Westacott — Abbotsham — Rickard's Down — Lake — Westward Ho!

7 miles. *Map — OS Explorer 139.*

When arriving by car take the road nearest to the sea and look for the cricket ground. There is a good car park at the Sunshine Leisure Park (£1 a day in '02) on the corner of Westbourne Terrace (GR 433 294) and a public car park along the Terrace on the right-hand side.

Having successfully completed that manoeuvre turn off along Westbourne Terrace and at the end meets the SW coast path. Turn left and stride out (no malingering among the ambling tourists) along the wide promenade with not surprisingly some splendid sea views. The inshore views are less spectacular so it is a case of eyes right except for those who derive pleasure from the sight of amusement arcades, candy floss and all the fun of the seaside. All such amenities are left behind on reaching Braddick's Holiday Centre allowing us to join the coast path in all its elemental beauty.

The path is to seaward of the beach huts and chalets. At Rock Nose enter

The Beach at Westward Ho!

National Trust land, Kiplings Tors, and on to Cornborough and Abbotsham Cliffs. The sandy beach gives way to shaley rock and soon the path becomes more rugged with lovely views both out to sea and inland over some extensive rural scenery - on a good day the best of all worlds for the dedicated walker. These attractions do inevitably take on a rather wild and more bracing characteristic when the wind and rain sweep in from the Atlantic. Seasoned walkers will be suitably equipped for all eventualities and will enjoy such a walk whatever the weather. The occasional walker might be well advised to pick a suitable day for coastal walking.

Under the better weather conditions (several days in most years!) Hartland point and the lighthouse are clearly visible and Clovelly harbour can be seen nestling in the foot of the cliffs. The first two walks in this book take in a few miles of less demanding stretches of coastline but nevertheless provide a useful insight into the wonders of coastal walking. (The third walk makes a useful introduction to the much tougher going along the north coast further along) The South West Way, to give it its proper name, is undoubtedly one of the great walking challenges in the country. Over 600 miles long, it includes some severe ups and downs much of which is along the north coast from Clovelly right down to Lands End. It would be nice to think that the walks in this book will inspire budding walkers to

Cornborough Cliffs

complete the whole way from Minehead to Poole.

However, to the present, pass the first footpath sign on Abbotsham Cliff (to Abbotsham Court) and climb the hill ahead. Once up carry on down and around, through a N.T. gateway and across a stream before once again climbing to a stile. On the descent a ravine can be seen in the valley. The path goes around the ravine (quite a good idea) and once the other side leave the coast path at the signpost and head inland uphill. At the top corner of the field turn right to a stile and the path which leads to Greencliff Farm. Turn left at the junction with the farm entrance and take the concrete road to the end and then turn right on to a narrow country road. Wend your way up the hill to the T-junction and turn left for Abbotsham. Before proceeding down the Abbotsham road turn round and take in the spectacular views across Cornborough Cliffs to the sea. On the way pass the entrance to Abbotswood farm and the elegant Lendon House a little further on.

Abbotsham soon hoves into sight with the village centre not far ahead where a rich range of amenities await. In this hub of activity can be found a Church; Chapel, Post Office Stores and a Village Hall but no pub — you have to walk a few yards down the road for that.

Like most of our Parish Churches, St. Helen's, is a lovely example of its kind and it is worthwhile spending a few minutes to enjoy the atmosphere and history of the place. The churchyard is maintained in immaculate condition and the church dignitaries (and possibly the residents) are justly proud of it. If time is available (and one should not be in too much of a hurry on these short walks) a tour of the tombstones will provide a fascinating insight into the village families through the ages.

The route out of the village is via the road signed for Westward Ho! but only for a very short distance before turning off left by the sign for the "Thatched Inn", Alas! Just before reaching this Mecca for thirsty travellers turn left again into Pump Lane, a narrow lane with an interesting mix of properties old and new. Where the roadway bears round to the right there is a RUPP immediately in front where the road carries on to the left.

Leave the roadway at this point and join the RUPP where a sign quite accurately reads "Unsuitable for motors". However it is not too bad under-foot and is pleasantly tree-lined. Naturally preferable to road walking there can be a slight problem in wet conditions when the outcropping rock surfaces are inclined to be slippery.

On reaching Rickard's Down at the top of the track turn left and almost at once turn right on to the Cornborough road. Major construction works are nearly complete for a new sewage treatment works to serve a large area of North Devon here and when operational should have no adverse effect on the passing walker. The works are on the inshore side of the road and thus any aerial evidence of their presence will be blown inland by the prevailing winds off the sea.

Further along the road the entrance to the Cornborough estate is passed. Evidently a place of some eminence, certainly in the past, all that can be seen from the road is the Lodge with a grassed triangle in front where an old oak tree flourishes. Under suitable weather conditions the triangle is an excellent place to sit for a drink and a bite.

Soon we come across a most unlikely development in so rural and area. Never let it be said this backwater is all about history for here at Lake there is sited an all-modern up-to-date Heliport. A major sewage works and a Heliport certainly puts it on the map although a few paces on and we are brought down to more earthy matters at the Duckhaven Stud. The walk

Westward Ho!

20

Abbotsham Church

clearly doesn't lack variety.

Just past the Stud there is a row of very expensive-looking modern properties having extensive views of the sea and Bideford in the distance. At the point where there is a right turn signed for Pusehill go through the gateway on the left which leads to a footpath between two rows of houses but soon to a path beside a lovely wooded gorge.

It is now downhill all the way into Westward Ho! Ignore the several tracks, which branch off the main one and simply keep going straight down the hill with views out to sea and Lundy Island right ahead.

On reaching the built-up area turn right along the tarmac roadway and re-join the coast path this time turning right. Carry on along the promenade and at "The Carousel" turn right into Westbourne Terrace and journey's end.

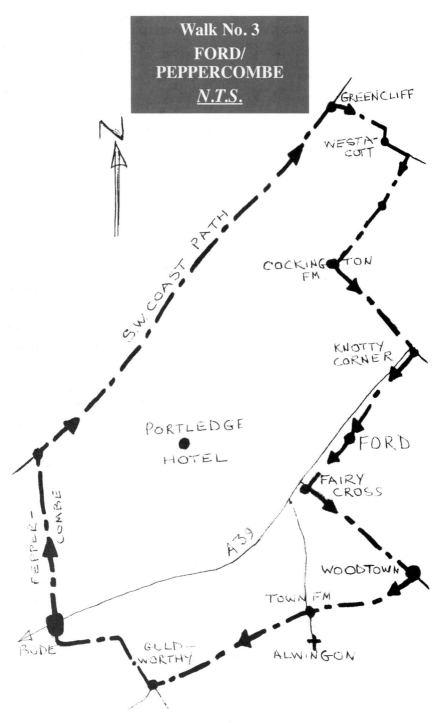

Walk No. 3
FORD/
PEPPERCOMBE
N.T.S.

N

GREENCLIFF

WESTA-
COTT

S.W. COAST PATH

COCKINGTON
FM

KNOTTY
CORNER

PORTLEDGE
HOTEL

FORD

FAIRY
CROSS

PEPPER-
COMBE

A39

WOODTOWN

TOWN FM

BUDE

GULD-
WORTHY

ALWINGON

BIDEFORD AREA WALK NO. 3

Ford — Woodtown — Alwington — Goldworthy — Horns Cross — Peppercombe — SW Coast Path — Greencliff — Cockington — Knotty Corner — Ford.

9 Miles. *Map — OS Explorer 126 or 139.*

This is the last of the three walks taking in sections of the South West Way (coast path).

Note 1. The walk does involve about 3 miles of the coast path which is more strenuous than in walks 1 and 2 and although no problem for the experienced walker it should not be attempted by anyone who is unfit particularly those with heart or respiratory problems.

Note 2. The walk also necessitates two crossings of the busy A39 both of which require good judgement and some athletic agility. Subject to these provisos it really is a glorious walk in some superb countryside and breath-taking coastal scenery.

There are no public parking facilities in Ford but the roadway through is quiet and wide with ample room to park anywhere between the Methodist Church and Giffords Ford Farm (GR408245)

Start out towards Fairy Cross and turn left there for Woodtown. Pass Moors Park farmhouse and from the top of the hill Woodtown can be seen across the valley — so does the hill beyond which you will be climbing later. However, reach Woodtown first. It is a small hamlet and attractive in the way of so many of these isolated settlements and no doubt and ideal place to live for the countryside lover.

On reaching the T-junction in Woodtown turn right to climb the hill referred to previously and note an interesting feature on the left—hand side as you leave the hamlet. It looks to be an old Parish pump which someone has taken a lot of time and trouble to renovate.

About half a mile along the road there is a crossroads at Town Farm where our route proceeds straight over to the road for Goldworthy and Horns Cross. However, just past the farm make a very slight diversion to the left for a visit to an absolute gem of a church. The Church of St. Andrew is the Parish Church of Alwington and has been in the patronage of the Pine-Coffin family since the 13th century. There is a great deal of historical evidence to fascinate the interested observer and a well-produced booklet to buy. Unfortunately, as a result of the age we live in the building has to be kept locked and anyone wishing to pay a well-worth visit should seek prior permission from the Church authorities or at Town Farm.

Alwington Church

Returning to the road turn left and pass West Dydon to a T-junction and then straight down the hill with Parkham Church in the distance. Bear right for Goldworthy and at West Goldworthy Farm take the road into Horns Cross. There is no need for a map or compass here — the "Coach and Horses" sign is prominently displayed immediately ahead on the far side of the A39.

At the "Stop" sign, do. The vehicles thundering along the trunk road will have no mercy on the jaywalker. For walkers wishing to replenish their victual supplies there is a Post Office Store on the near side just round to the left, which can be visited before crossing the road.

Should the crossing of the A39 prove to be too nerve racking or harrowing comfort and suitable restoratives may be purchased at the "Coach and Horses" to be partaken in very pleasant and relaxed surroundings. Either way proceed down the lane beside the pub to take the right-hand of the two diverging footpaths where the lane ends. This right-hand path is in fact a wide, well-surfaced track down to Peppercombe with the huge gorge on the left. The gorge and the slopes on the right are a mass of dense woodland. A seat, thoughtfully provided by the National Trust no doubt, makes a good place to sit for a few minutes to take in the scenery and listen to the birds in concert.

It is quite a surprise suddenly to come upon an old thatched cottage in this idyllic setting and a little further down the track to see one or two more such properties among the trees on the left. Holidaymakers who rent them must have a memorable vacation because a few yards more and there is the first sight of the sea.

At the bottom of the track just before an old stone bridge over the combe and an old stone barn with a spreading copper beach tree there is a small gateway on the right. This leads directly on to the coast path.

For keen bathers who fancy a dip before continuing the walk there is a gateway on the far side of the bridge with a sign pointing to the beach. Such hardy souls are wished the best of luck.

While climbing the path up to the top of the cliff above the combe take a peep backwards to admire the magnificent views. If nothing else it should provide inspiration for undertaking the three miles of tough switchback walking which lies ahead. As one would expect the coastal scenery is wonderful, on a good day it is possible to see for miles. When the winds sweep in from America there is rather less to see but the effect is quite exhilarating.

The SW Way considering its length and exposure to the elements is maintained in remarkably good condition. It is somewhat narrow in some places so reasonable care is needed particularly where the cliffs are sheer and high. In a number of places the path is so steep that steps have been cut into the hillsides and which, although uncomfortable to use, are no doubt preferable to sliding down a few hundred feet into a stream or gorse bush.

The sea views are so magnificent that after a time they can tend to have a mesmerising effect on the viewer and induce a kind of visual indigestion in which case cast an occasional glance inland where the rural scenery is equally attractive.

For walkers who have recently done Walk 2 Greencliff will be a familiar sight and probably a welcome one since the coast walk will have taken longer than the actual distance might suggest. A clearly marked sign-

The Coast at Greencliff

post is confirmation that it is indeed Greencliff and it is at this point we turn our backs on the sea and go straight up the hill. At the top of the field turn right beside the fence and cross the stile, which leads to Greencliff, farm. Turn left along the concrete farm entrance road and where it joins the county road turn right (as in walk 2). The lane winds its way up to a T—junction where, on this walk, we turn right to pass Westacott Farm. On reaching the entrance to Cockington Farm turn left down a pleasant leafy lane beside Cockington Plantation.

The lane ends abruptly at the A39. A sign with the words "Give Way" greets motorists but which under the circumstances is advice to walkers too and not to be faulted. There is a slight problem here. Instead of the lane going straight across as it once did it is now for obvious reasons a staggered crossing. Consequently it is necessary to turn right and walk along the verge before reaching the point where we cross to Knotty Corner. Needless to say it is critically important to take great care in crossing.

Once safely across turn right and enjoy the relief at walking along a quiet lane and quite soon past some good-looking modern properties into Ford. For anyone with the time and interest there is a Water Garden, which is open to the public, just before the area where the car will be parked. All that remains is to be re-united with the vehicle and join the merciless metal-clad warriors roaring along the A39.

The Track down to Peppercombe

The Cliffs at Peppercombe

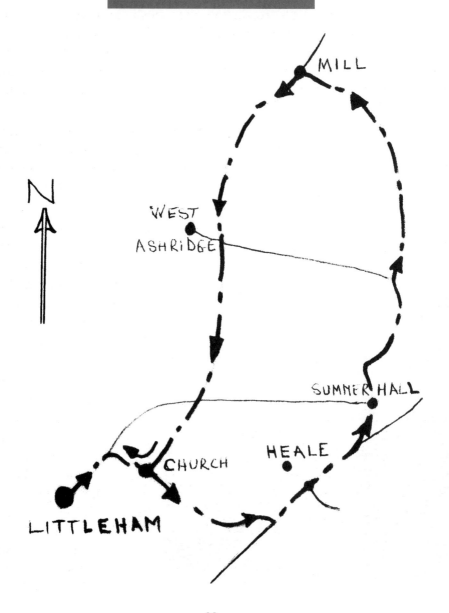

MILL

N

WEST
ASHRIDGE

SUMNER HALL

HEALE

CHURCH

LITTLEHAM

WALK NO. 4

Littleham — Church — Edge Mill — Summerhill — Mill — West Ashridge — Littleham.

5 Miles. *Map — OS Explorer 126 or 139.*

There are no "real" roads into Littleham village and the best approach from both the Bideford and Torrington directions is to drive to Landcross and turn off there on to the road signed for Littleham. Two miles along this road there is a crossroads with the narrow lane on the right being the way into Littleham. Parking is available in the roadway into the "Crealock Arms" or in the pub car park by arrangement with the landlord (GR437233).

Leave the pub approach road and turn right for a few yards before turning left where the sign indicates the way to the Church. Pass the Methodist Church and a cluster of old and newer properties which blend in well together. Look out for the sign on a fence indicating the lane down to the Church.

Follow the signs for Littleham Church through a small enclave of lovely rural surroundings with a number of smart, expensive looking properties dotted about. The lane ends at the Church Car Park which is quite spacious

Littleham Church

and would be a good place to leave a car but for the fact that the lane down to it is narrow and not in very good condition.

The Church, firmly locked, is of traditional stone and of post-Conquest vintage set in a delightfully peaceful spot but seemingly remote from its customers. Perhaps the ecclesiastical architects of the time considered the local peasantry would benefit from a long walk to church followed by a lengthy sermon. Physical effort and spiritual uplift together would thus provide the advantages of both worlds. The size of car park suggests the present day worshippers have dispensed with the former.

Adjoining the Church is a quite magnificent property which presumably was once a Vicarage although it looks altogether too palatial for that. If indeed it was originally the home of Incumbents then one can only envy their lifestyle. To dwell in such splendour with a house full of servants with the job of writing sermons designed to "teach the rustic moralist to die" (as Thomas Gray put it) could not have been too onerous.

Sticking to the physical effort our walk goes through the churchyard beside the Church itself and opens out at the far end on to a track where we turn right to climb over a stile into the field. Keep to the hedge on the right and clamber over a stile at the other end of the field. Turn down left here to enjoy a superb walk along a metalled track providing views across the valley before reaching some dense woodland.

The track takes a sharp turn to the right eventually with a fork ahead at which point take the left hand leg down the steep hill to join the county road.

Turn left along the road (which is most likely the one driven along earlier in the day) for about half a mile. The road is parallel and quite close to the R.Yeo with trees both sides. It is quite a lovely avenue walk although somewhat spoiled by the traffic. There is not a great deal of it but what there is tends to move very fast.

Turn off left on to the narrow, but safer, lane at the Old Toll House and climb up past Summerhall and the overhanging conker tree before turning off at Spinney cottage. After the garage of the last property the lane becomes a RUPP, unsuitable for motors, and thereby a treat to use. The track does become rather rough and overgrown in places but does provide the occasional view across to Landcross- if you can take your eyes off the places where the feet are landing.

The track comes to an end at a narrow county road on a corner. Turn right and plod along the road and at the entrance to Ashridge Barton leave the road for the rough track, which drops, steeply to the Mill at the bottom.

Turn left there to find the RUPP shown on the OS Map. Climb this metalled track which is rough to begin with but eventually gives way to a grassy surface and, again, is inclined to be overgrown in places.

Old Toll House

Where the track meets the county road at the entrance to West Ashridge carry straight on past Heale Farm to a T junction. Go almost straight across on to a footpath for a short distance where it meets the gateway into Littleham churchyard. Return via the churchyard path and the lane back into the village.

Although only a short walk this one is full of variety and interest and of course an excellent hostelry at the end of it for those walkers so inclined.

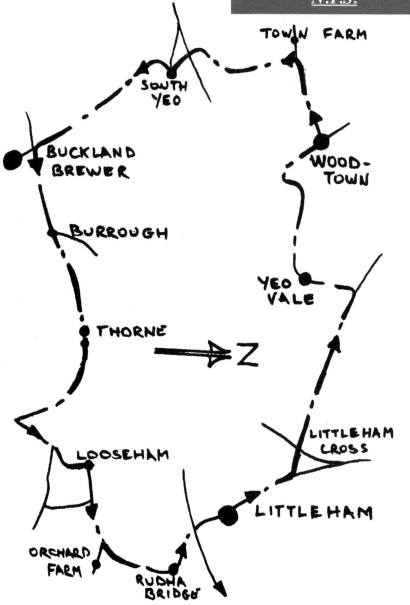

TOWN FARM

SOUTH YEO

BUCKLAND BREWER

WOOD-TOWN

BURROUGH

YEO VALE

THORNE

Z

LITTLEHAM CROSS

LOOSEHAM

LITTLEHAM

ORCHARD FARM

RUDHA BRIDGE

WALK NO. 5

Littleham — Littleham Cross — Yeo Vale — Woodtown — Town Farm — South Yeo — Bowden Cross — Buckland Brewer — Burrough — Thorne — Rudha Bridge — Littleham.

8 Miles. *Maps — OS Explorer 126 or 139.*

Begin the walk as for Walk 4 in the Crealock Arms area. This time turn left on leaving the road into the Crealock Arms and walk up the hill making for Littleham Cross. At the South West Water reservoir compound turn left and continue straight across at Moor Head Cross along the road which is signed for Abbotsham and Clovelly.

This stretch of road is straight and quiet with a narrow plantation of fine oak and ash trees on the left-hand side all of which makes for a very pleasant walk. A few yards past the point where the plantation ends look for the cleverly concealed "Bridleway" sign on the left. It is at spot level 117 on the OS Map and beside the entrance to Winscott Barton.

One of the interesting aspects of these country walks is the quite sudden change of environment which can occur within a few steps. The road just walked along is agreeably rural but once on the bridleway the walker is in wild, splendid isolation. Nature's rich diversity may well be appreciated more through the eyes than those parts of the anatomy, which operate below the knees in such surroundings, but then we cannot always have something for nothing. On this particular track there are one or two irritants, which afflict the passer-by. The surface is very lumpy and uneven with some large stones lurking among grassy tufts and ruts, which readily fill with water and form miniature rivulets in wet weather. While the feet tread warily through the mire the overgrowing and out-reaching brambles and hedges seek to entwine themselves round the lower leg with loving embrace. Under these circumstances gaiters are an important part of the equipment although billhooks are not really essential. However, the properly equipped walker will thoroughly enjoy the untamed beauty of the bridleway and like all good things of course it does not come to an end.

It opens up at the bottom on to a farm complex. At the T-junction turn right to pass through the farm buildings at Yeo Vale and turn right again on reaching the county road which leads to Woodtown. Pass a most attractive thatched cottage and an all-up-to-date telephone box, which possibly is working, and arrive in Woodtown.

Bridge over the River Yeo

Turn left at the T-junction on to the road signed for Alwington which will be familiar to those who completed Walk 3. The hamlet is small and compact so the time between arrival and departure is very brief, however there are two quite interesting features to observe in passing. Note the wall mounted Post Box of VR vintage on the corner house since there are moves afoot to have these things listed for historic reasons. The other feature, as referred to in Walk 3, is the restored village pump on the left hand side of the road on the way through.

Plod on up the hill out of Woodtown and on this walk look out for a sign on the left just before Town Farm, which reads "Unsuitable for Motor Vehicles". This is shown on the OS map as a RUPP and, apart from walkers who wish to make a worthwhile diversion to see Alwington church, is the route to take. It is a wide downhill track fairly easy on the foot but does become a little rougher towards the bottom but is offset by the pleasure of walking through an avenue of mature trees.

Cross the bridge over the River Yeo and the main road ahead and join the narrow lane up to South Yeo. This short stretch of hill is noticeable for the huge, magnificent old beech trees on the left-hand side. Turn left on reaching the T junction and set out on the walk to Bowden Cross for nearly a mile of what may be fairly described as a typically English lane.

At Bowden Cross it is decision time. The walker may wish to make the short diversion into Buckland Brewer in order to take advantage of the wide range of facilities on offer. These include a Post Office Store, a butchers shop and that indispensable amenity of any English village — a pub — "The Coach and Horses". However, it should be pointed out that walk 6 actually begins in Buckland Brewer so these delights can be deferred for another day. In which case on arriving at Bowden Cross turn left on to the main road.

This road is quite a busy one at times. It has the disadvantage of being somewhat bendy and although providing some splendid views on each side allows the motorist very little time in which to see a pedestrian, so keep eyes and ears alert. Fortunately there is not far to go. On a left-hand bend in the road amid a small group of houses at Burrough a narrow lane turns off on the right. Just look for the sign "Not suitable for heavy goods vehicles" and leave the main road. It is certainly not good for lorries but is a joy for the walker.

This lane is really very narrow all the way to the small group of impressive properties at Thorne and thereafter becomes even narrower to form a lovely avenue, which steepens rapidly towards the end as it drops down to the R. Duntz. This walk alongside the river to the bridge through extensive natural woodland is not very far but really is quite glorious.

Once over the bridge and leaving the river behind inevitably means some uphill work along what is still a narrow lane. The avenues, which have been so prominent earlier in the walk, now give way to the more traditional Devon hedgerows which in places grow high and wide.

Further along towards Looseham Farm the countryside becomes more open allowing for some fine views with Littleham itself visible on the hill away to the north. One unusual development along here catches the eye. A new wide driveway fenced on each side has been laid out with two signs at the entrance, which read, "Memorial Avenue", and underneath, "Foot and Mouth 2001". The bitter memories of that disaster will long be with the farming fraternity.

Looseham is a large farm settlement passed along the way. Just keep going over the stream in the valley and begin the steep climb up to the Orchard Farm turning. Keep to the left and drop sharply to the area where the River Duntz and Yeo meet at Rudha Bridge and Orleigh Mills —

Memorial Avenue — Looseham

another lovely spot. Cross the bridge and enjoy the last sight of the River Yeo on this walk before crossing the main (and quite busy) road. Go straight across and take the narrow, steep hill up to Littleham. The lane is winding as well as narrow but there are a number of passing places for cars which do provide sanctuary for the walker as well. Apart from these passing places two cars cannot pass each other but there is just about width enough for a pedestrian and car to pass provided the latter is not averse to blending into the wild, thorny hedge. The lane does widen as it nears the village where it passes through the (many) Langdons.

Within a few minutes journey's end will be in sight and, if the itinerary has been appropriately planned, the thirsty traveller will be in time to take advantage of the excellent facilities at the Crealock Arms.

Woodtown

By the bridge over the River Duntz

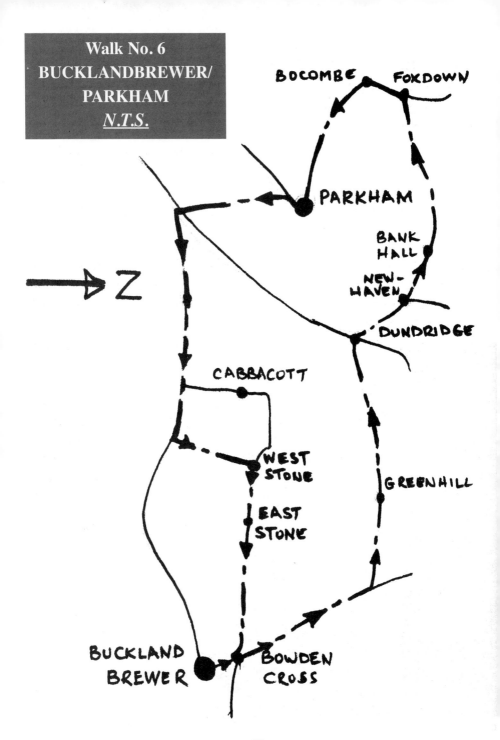

Walk No. 6
BUCKLANDBREWER/
PARKHAM
N.T.S.

BOCOMBE
FOXDOWN
PARKHAM
BANK HALL
NEW-HAVEN
DUNDRIDGE
CABBACOTT
WEST STONE
EAST STONE
GREENHILL
BUCKLAND BREWER
BOWDEN CROSS

Z

WALK NO. 6

Buckland Brewer — Bowden Cross — Greenhill — Dundridge —Newhaven — Bank Hall — Foxdown — Bocombe — Parkham — Babeleigh — Buckland Brewer.

7 Miles. *Map — OS Explorer 126 or 139.*

There is no public car park in the village so either park by the roadside (the road is quite wide) near the church or seek consent from the landlord of the local pub (GR419209).

Once satisfactorily parked set off up the road past the church to Bowden Cross and then on to the road signed for Tuckingmill. The OS map does indicate a public footpath across fields to the RUPP but there is no evidence of its existence on the ground. However, it is only a short distance to the point where the RUPP joins the road. Keep going past a pair of houses to the two bungalows a little further along and turn onto the RUPP mid-way between them.

One of the better RUPPS — Greenhill

The track is fine and wide to begin with but does become somewhat boggy and it is advisable to have gaiters available for this stretch. To begin with it is downhill to where a stream crosses and from there the surface becomes somewhat firmer and easier. A note of caution- do be careful where the feet touch down lest your boots gather malodorous samples of where a horse has recently been in motion.

The vegetation along this track provides an insight into the way our mild, murky West Country weather encourages lush and rapid growth. Just beware of the overhanging bramble seeking to caress your brow, the nettles to tickle your arms and legs or the wild rose rambling to embrace you. There is plenty of evidence of these natural phenomena along here. An interesting thing for the observant walker to keep a look out for is the gaps opposite each other in the hedges where nocturnal animals have their crossing places.

Eventually the track becomes well cared for as far as the entrance to Cabbacott Farm but thereafter tends to go native again. It finally ends at a tarmac lane, which extends down a very steep hill where the muscles in the calves become extended. Cross straight over the main road at the bottom of the hill to join another track for a little way, cross the stone bridge in the valley and make for the county road at the top of the hill ahead.

The walk thus far has been excellent and there are more delights to come all the way into Parkham. On reaching the county road turn right and at the T-junction take the left hand road signed for Goldworthy and Horns Cross.

Bear right, still on the Horns Cross road at the rather attractive hamlet of Newhaven and keep on up the hill as far as the entrance to Bank Hall. Turn left into the narrow entrance track, which soon opens out on to a lovely area beside the stream and follow the track right round to the right past the house. Bank Hall does sound rather impressive but is in fact quite a small typically rural cottage complete with roses round the door (well, Virginia creeper actually). On the area of grass in front of the cottage a maturing conker tree grows with a wrought iron seat beneath. It provides a nice touch but whether it is solely for the use of occupiers or for the benefit of itinerant passers-by is not made clear. For the avoidance of doubt anyone thinking about pausing at this delightful spot for a snack would be well advised to sit on the footbridge over the adjacent stream.

Just past the cottage the track meets the footpath, which extends more or less from Foxdown to Horns Cross. At this T "junction" there is a short post in the garden border with yellow footpath marker arrows pointing in each direction. Take the left hand path between a garage and stable block. Go through the old rickety gate ahead (manipulate carefully to avoid a hernia) and through a second, more modern and less difficult, gateway at the far end of the field.

Accurate navigation is essential from this gate for the next quarter of a mile or so. Make for the hump in the middle of the field and then half right for an oak tree in the hedge. The tree is bigger than those around it so should be fairly easy to pick out. It is important to do so because the stile we need to cross is tucked away in the hedge just to the right of the tree.

Once over the stile the problems are not over. The route is not way-marked but it is essential to get down into the woods on the left straight-away. Do not follow the edge of the woodland. The woods are quite thick with a stream running along the bottom with a boggy area beside it. The knack is to keep above the bog and walk parallel to the stream with eyes on the stream. There is a perfectly good footbridge part way along but unfortunately it is obscured by a large tree, which has fallen in front of it. Hence, look for this tree and either climb over or under it but on no account overshoot because the terrain ahead is exceedingly difficult.

Having succeeded in locating the footbridge cross over it and take the rough path up the hill for a short distance before turning off right on to what is euphemistically shown on the OS Map and on the ground as a public footpath. It is very narrow and confined between two fence lines each heavily overgrown which presents the walker with a challenge to fight his/her way through a tanglement of bramble, wild rose and sundry other natural hazards as described earlier.

The path is not very long and the walker may even emerge unscathed on to the narrow roadway, which, on turning left, leads to a lovely walk beside woods and a stream, which ends at Foxdown. This is another beautiful

Bocombe Mill

41

hamlet, very rural and very peaceful and the road from here to Bocombe Mill is similarly through delightful, wooded country.

At the top of the hill bear left at the Y junction. At the T-junction, some way further on turn first right and almost immediately left along Chapel Road into Parkham.

Turn right to join the main highway through the village. First of all St. Jame's Church with a rather dark and forbidding exterior but with a light and interesting inside. The present structure is on the site of an earlier Anglo-Saxon church and is mainly 15th century. The builders seem to have been either very particular in their choice of materials or shrewd business-men keen to drive a hard bargain. They shopped around as we might say. The font has a surround of "Barum" ("Barnstaple" to the uninitiated) tiles and the arches are constructed on Lundy granite columns.

From the church continue along the road for Buckland Brewer. Pass a garage and at a "School" sign just as you may be despairing of ever finding that indispensable amenity of any English village worth its name— the Bell Inn comes into view. For those who partake of such facilities the Bell Inn is a good example of its kind. There is a pleasant, relaxed atmosphere with good ale and excellent menu on offer. Parkham itself exudes the same sort of friendly air about the place but just remember before spending too long there that you have another couple of miles to walk and a clear head is a distinct advantage.

Skirt around the inn to take the side road as far as the somewhat luxuri-ous looking Penhaven Hotel at which point turn off right along the well-surfaced track alongside the hotel. Where the track bends round to the left take the footpath on the right, which is narrow and enclosed by thick hedges. Pass Easter View, a fine house in lovely grounds, as far as the part-ing of the ways.

Cross the stile immediately in front of you and go down over the field with the hedge on the left. At the barn at the bottom look for another stile (look hard because it is not readily apparent) beside a concrete block exten-sion to the old barn and carry on down over the field. At the bottom of this field cross the stile in the corner and down the steps to the road.

Turn left to go over the "main" road to take the lesser lane signed for Buckland Brewer and keep going for about half a mile, the main feature being the majestic avenue of mature beech trees in one section.

Pass the sign for Cabbacott on the left and a little way further along turn off on to the RUPP with the "Unsuitable for Motors" sign at the entrance. The RUPP ends at West Stone Farm. Bear right to face a sort of T-junction of tracks with a farm gate on the right and an unusable stile on the right-hand side. Go through the gateway (purists may prefer to negotiate the stile) and follow the hedge round to the left to the opening on to an arable field.

The OS map clearly shows a public footpath across the field itself but most dedicated lovers of the countryside will prefer to keep to the hedge on the left. On the far side of the field there is a stile to cross which may be overgrown but is sited about 50 yards down from the corner and not too difficult to find.

Keep close to the hedge in the second field and locate the gateway on to the road just beyond East Stone Farm. Turn right and proceed along the lane to the now familiar Bowden Cross. From here all that remains is a short stroll down through the village to the car and the end of a super 7 miles walking.

Bankhall

Walk No. 7
MONKLEIGH/ BUCKLAND BREWER
<u>*N.T.S.*</u>

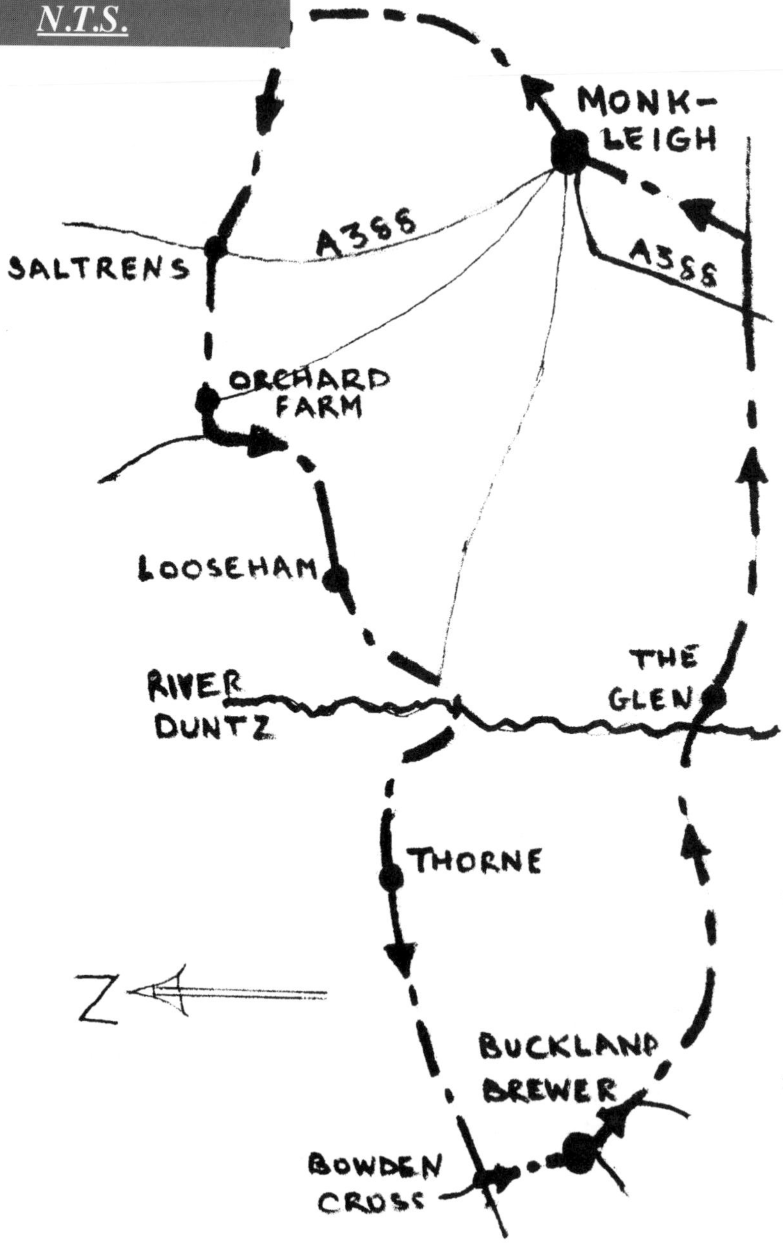
MONK-
LEIGH
A388
A388
SALTRENS
ORCHARD
FARM
LOOSEHAM
RIVER
DUNTZ
THE
GLEN
THORNE
N
BUCKLAND
BREWER
BOWDEN
CROSS

WALK NO. 7

Monkleigh — Rendle's Down — Saltrens — Orchard Farm — Looseham — Thorne — Buckland Brewer — The Glen — Combe — Higher Culleigh — Monkleigh

8 Miles. *Map — OS Explorer 126.*

There is ample parking in the area around the Village Hall area (GR 457 208)

The walk is almost entirely on tarmac there being just one short length of RUPP and a public footpath across fields for the finale. Begin by going up the hill to the village centre and at the T-junction turn off right on to the road signed for Weare Gifford.

Pass the village school and a short distance further along take the lane (signed as a "No through Road") to Rendle's Down. It is a pleasant and quiet leafy lane with a solitary, gnarled old oak tree standing like a lone sentinel watching over the road at one spot. Note the superb distant views of Bideford on passing the entrance to Ley Farm. From this point drop down the hill to Rendle's Down and at the bottom turn left on to the RUPP with the "Unfit for Motors" warning sign.

As RUPP's go this one is quite good particularly the first part uphill

where the surface is grassy and level although the downhill side is some-what rougher due to loose stones underfoot. The water trickling down the side suggests that in wet weather walking boots will be effectively water-cooled. The RUPP ends beside a most attractive old stone and rendered house set in a quite dense wooded area with a stream running (at times rushing) through. Any illusions induced by the beauty are likely to be brought down to earth a little further along the lane by the sight of what can best be described as a disused vehicle graveyard. It would be difficult to suggest a more delightful place for so incongruous a "development". However, the thing to do is to keep the eyes firmly to the right where the beauty remains unadulterated.

Not much further down the lane another interesting phenomenon under the heading of "Waste Disposal" comes into view — well not exactly into view because very little is visible above ground and it is only likely to be detected via the nose. It is the now rapidly ageing sewage treatment plant serving the hamlet of Saltrens, which in spite of its antiquity seems to perform the necessary function quite adequately. At least the designer had the foresight to build it a long way from the houses. Out of sight, out of mind was probably the guiding philosophy.

Annery

After so much excitement in so short a distance it is something of an anti-climax to arrive in Saltrens itself. A neat and tidy little hamlet astride the A388, which need not detain us, any longer than it takes to walk through it. On arriving at the main road turn right for a few yards and then cross over to take the lane, which begins, just before the last house in the place. This lane is a good example of Devon highways — a thick hedge each side and very little room between them.

At the T junction opposite Orchard Farm turn right for a few yards as far as the grass "island" T junction then turn left on to the unsigned lane. Walkers who have completed Walk 5 will recognise familiar ground. However, this time it will be in the opposite direction, which means that instead of toiling up the very steep hill you may enjoy the luxury of free-wheeling down it this time.

Pass the busy Looseham Farm and the interesting memorial drive created to commemorate the 2001 Foot and Mouth disaster, both of which are described in Walk 5.

The open countryside now gives way to some truly glorious woodland scenery. First of all, as the road drops down to the river there is a well-managed wood of oak and ash trees on the right hand side. The road bends

46

round past an old stone cottage to a bridge over the River Duntz in one of those spots it is a pleasure to come across. Once over the river the road rises very steeply up through overhanging, wild and lush woodland. It is a long climb but the steepest stretch is over on reaching two magnificent beech trees forming a dense canopy above the road. Thereafter the gradient is a lot more gentle although there is still a long haul ahead. The narrow road becomes almost totally confined between high hedges and although there may be rather less to see the area reverberates to the raucous screeching of numerous pheasants. To be walking along a peaceful pastoral by-way engrossed in the beauty of it all and to turn up pheasants is liable to induce a nasty state of shock to the unwary although the awful racket suggests the birds are even more startled at being disturbed. They are quite ungainly, awkward birds and in this area there are a whole lot of them.

Thorne is the next milestone in our travels. Like so many of these remote settlements it comprises a number of modern and older properties, which blend in well together and above all do not straggle in ribbon development fashion. They form a very attractive compact group.

We are still going uphill and in fact will be doing so all the way to Bowden Cross but first reach the main road at Burrough. Turn left and after a short distance decide upon the way forward. The OS map clearly shows a public right of way across the fields on the left, which leads to the centre of Buckland Brewer. However, maintenance of footpaths in the area leaves a good deal to be desired and although there is a signpost indicating the line of a public right of way the going may be too muddy or rough under some weather conditions. The alternative is to carry on along the road to Bowden's Cross, turn left and drop down into the village. The road is quite busy and bendy so care is needed but the distance is not particularly great. The individual walker must decide which route to take.

Either way the way ahead is straight down through Buckland Brewer past (or otherwise, according to taste) "The Coach and Horses". The lane out of the village is downhill past a line of fine oak trees on the left-hand side and once again through an area densely populated by pheasants. After the best part of a mile the road reaches another glorious place at "The Glen" on the River Duntz. It is a tricky bit of the road for the motorist but superb for the tramp.

Cross the river by the old, narrow stone bridge and be prepared for a stiff uphill climb - the double black arrow on the OS map will confirm the nature of the brute. At the top (while pausing for a breather) look back to admire the splendid view of Buckland Brewer on the hill beyond. The

Leaving Buckland Brewer

narrow road continues past Combe to end at the A388 which should be crossed with due care on to an equally narrow lane signed for Monkleigh Pottery and Torrington.

A little way down the lane just after the entrance to Higher Culleigh begin the search for a footpath on the left. Look for the first power line pole in the hedge. The footpath begins at the gateway beside the pole. There is in fact a FP sign on the near side but it coyly hides its message in the foliage of the hedge. Having located the gateway manipulate the actual gate with some thought for your future welfare. A strong man will manage it easily enough but the rest of us need to be careful.

Once in the field cross it to another gateway straight ahead. This gate is probably an imported variety because unlike most North Devon farm gates it opens quite easily. It also differs from most in that the top rail is ornamentally festooned with barbed wire. Follow the fence line to the stile and the hedge the other side round as far as a wide gap between fences. The village hall of Monkleigh is visible from this point: it is the last building on the right and a short walk up over the field brings the walk to a finish.

Looseham

Frithelstock

Walk No. 8
WEARE GIFFORD/ EAST-THE-WATER
N.T.S.

EAST-THE-
WATER
BIDEFORD
RAILWAY
STATION
N
WOODVILLE
GAMMATON
MOOR CROSS
R. TORRIDGE
TARKA TRAIL
HALLSPILL
VENTON
ANNERY
KILN
PARK
WEARE
GIFFORD
CAR
PARK

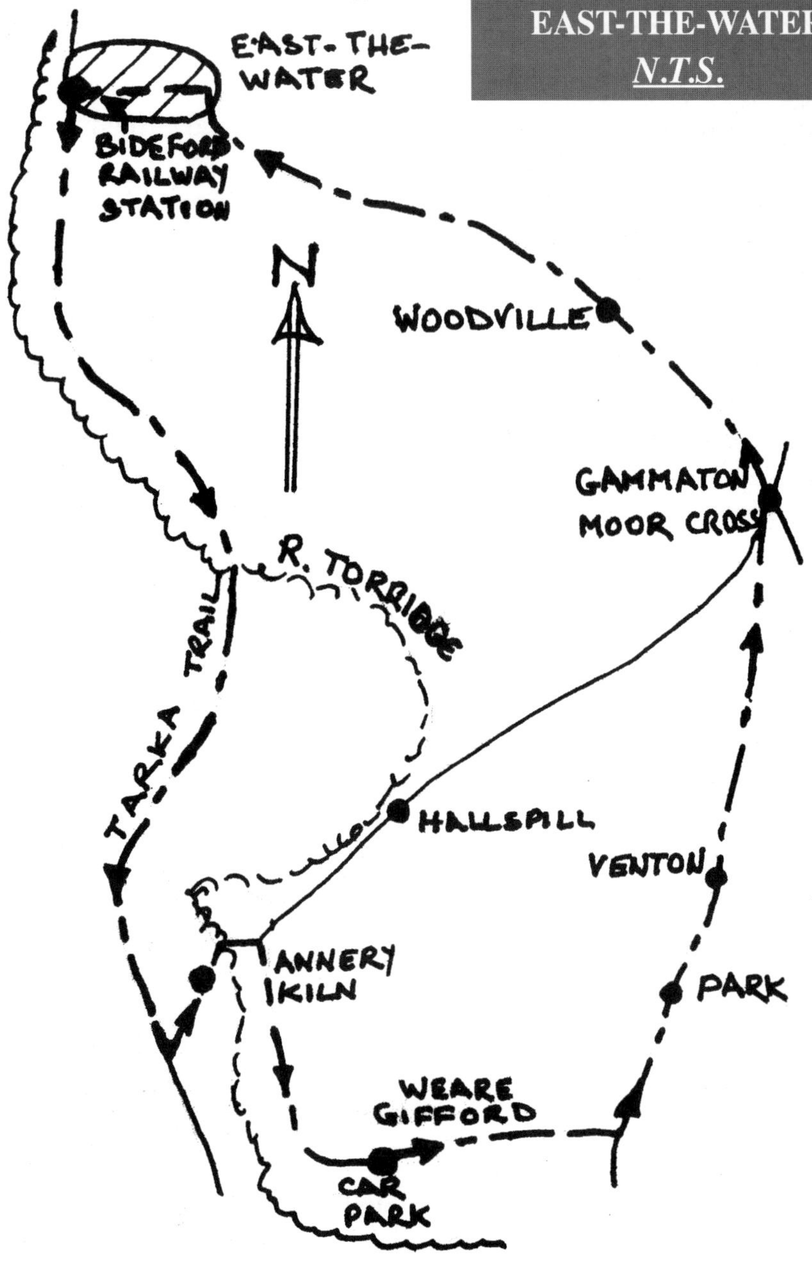

WALK NO.8

Weare Gifford — Venton — Gammaton Moor Cross — Woodville — East-The-Water — Tarka Trail (South) — Annery Kiln — Weare Gifford.

9 Miles. *Map — OS Explorer 126 or 139.*

If driving from the Bideford direction use the A386 and turn off to Weare Gifford over Halfpenny Bridge. From Torrington turn off the A386 on to the road opposite the church (passing the Dartington Glass Factory). Park at the village recreation ground (GR470222) or by arrangement with the landlord of the "Cyder Presse" (GR478220)

To begin the walk from the recreation ground car park cross the road at the east end of the car park and use the wide track through some lovely light woodland and drop down on to the narrow lane at the far end. To start from the "Cyder Presse" just turn off the "main" road to the narrow lane on the right and begin the climb. Join those who have started at the recreation ground and make the long steady ascent to Park Farm.

Just past Park Farm ignore the right-hand fork signed for Cleave and bear left on the lane leading up to Venton, a rather extensive enterprise of agricultural/industrial appearance. With rising height views over an increasingly wide area of somewhat featureless countryside are noticeable. The predominant feature would appear to be the network of National Grid powerlines, which stretch way out into the infinite distance. However, these things do not detract from the pleasure of walking in any way, it is just different from the rest of the area.

On arrival at the 3 way cross bear right to the main road at Gammaton Moor and turn left there on to the Bideford road. Unfortunately it is not possible to use the track shown on the map as going to Beara Farm because doing so would avoid the necessity to walk the fairly busy road into East-the- Water. Vigilance is the order of the day along this two-mile stretch particularly on the sharp bends, which occur. At least it is a downhill walk all the way giving some fine views of Bideford and the estuary right out to Baggy Point.

The 30mph sign signals the end of the ordeal at East-the-Water where the rural environment gives way abruptly to the encroaching urban development. At the T-junction industrial Bideford stretches out on both sides in front but on turning left is soon behind you. Pass through (rapidly)

Gammaton Moor Cross

the unimaginative, uninspired modern housing development along the Gammaton road and at the roundabout turn left on to Torrington Lane. Keep going down the hill bearing right at the bottom to enter the 20mph zone.

At the old Bideford Railway Station it is all change again — not trains, just surroundings and entirely for the better. Go on to the platform (no platform ticket required now and no timetable to worry about) and turn left beside the old rolling stock, now preserved, on to the Tarka Trail. The station building is now the office of the North Devon Coast and Countryside Service where information is available as well as refreshments.

What now follows is a delightful contrast with what has gone before. One of the many pleasures of these rural walks is the degree of variation in scenery and surroundings, which are often encountered in a short distance. After the rather moorland-like landscape up to Gammaton Moor Cross and the road walk into East-the-Water the Tarka Trail introduces an estuarine

Bideford Old Bridge

aspect into the proceedings. The trail along the old railway line follows the tidal reaches of the River Torridge all the way to Weare Gifford apart from the section at Landcross, which cuts out a large loop in the course of the river.

The fine river views are partially obstructed in a few places by the rapidly maturing lush tree and shrub growth which itself adds to the overall attractiveness. Superlatives readily come to mind in so many of our rural settings and in this case to describe the Tarka Trail as breathtaking is no exaggeration.

The inland view to begin with has a strangely different appeal all of its own. Quite a large area is now derelict and heavily overgrown with ruins of old industrial buildings dotted all over the place. These relics of recent enterprises appearing forlornly above the tangled undergrowth, in spite of their sad and sorry appearance, are oddly enough not offensive to the eye.

On the riverside at one point there is an entry on to the salt marshes with an interesting explanatory board giving detailed information about the existence of the Plume Moth and the Springtail, which apparently are thriving residents of the marshes. The casual walker may wonder what on earth these things are and question their choice of housing habitat but be full of admiration for their stoicism in preferring such a windswept, tide-washed place to settle and, presumably, raise a family.

The nature of the walking is, as one would expect on an old railway line, virtually level made easier by the tight and even surface which has been laid for the benefit of the walker and cyclists. One small problem, which can arise from the mixing of cyclists and pedestrians, is the biker who comes up astern of the walker unawares. A surprising number of bicycles are not equipped with bells (a legal requirement) and their silent arrival by your side can be quite disconcerting.

Just under a mile from Bideford Station the railway line crosses the River Torridge by, not surprisingly, a bridge. This is a place where you will want to spend some time enthralled by the sublime views up and down-stream of the upper reaches of the tidal river. Your stay will no doubt be accompanied by a multi-clicking of camera shutters. Only rarely can such

Upstream view from the Old Railway Bridge

54

stunning views be seen.

The next half a mile along the track has yet more interest albeit very different things to see. Through Pillmouth it is in a deep tree-lined cutting leading to the bridge under the main road (A386) at Landcross. The bridge itself is a fine example of railway engineering still in excellent condition in spite of the constant pounding from the heavy traffic above. Not far along there is another example of the old railway engineer's skill in the form of a long, curved tunnel, which took the railway under the A386 and A388.

The Old Manor House, Weare Gifford

The brick lining to the soffit of the arch looks to be as good as the day it was built. The tunnel is now lit for the benefit of the walkers and cyclists. Just beyond the far end of the tunnel where the track passes close to the main road the travellers may take advantage of a small picnic area that is if he/she does not worry too much about the noise of traffic above. A little further along there is a much larger picnic site beside the river which is

55

probably preferable to the smaller one.

It is nearing the time to leave Tarka to his own delights and the place to do so is where a field gate abuts on to the main road. There is a stone on the approach side bearing the name, in over-ornate lettering "Weare Gifford". A few paces along there is a truly eye-opening thing rather like a modern, metal totem pole with all manner of lettering and obscure shapes on it. No doubt it has some local significance but it will have served its purpose if it provides a reminder that this is the place to leave the Tarka Trail.

A road sign here indicates it is 2 miles to Weare Gifford which may seem curious because the first houses of the village are clearly visible just over the river, a matter of a few hundred yards away. The long trek through this elasticated-string-bean of a place will confirm the sign's accuracy however.

Immediately outside the gateway referred to above a narrow lane leaves the main road to pass under the Tarka Trail on the way to the village. First of all, before crossing the river lies Annery Kiln, a huge stone structure having more the appearance of a fortress than a kiln but a lime kiln it once was. It was a very large example of its kind and even now looks impressive in spite of crumbling stonework and a great deal of overgrowth!

Cross Halfpenny Bridge (no tolls to pay now) and enter the long straggling village that has no centre and is unlike almost any other village that comes to mind. Perhaps a "linear settlement" might be a more appropriate (if cumbersome) description. The road is close to the river bank at first and although the river at most times is a delightful sight on occasions it can become a swollen torrent which disgorges huge volumes of water into the village itself.

Keep plodding. Weare Gifford may seem endless but it really does end eventually. An interesting feature well worth a diversionary visit is the church of Holy Trinity, a small squat building and tower. Its appearance is more of ageless solidity rather than architectural grace but the interior is everything we have come to expect of our Parish Churches. It is rare to find stone effigies in so small a church but this one has some well-preserved figures of Sir Walter and Alice Gifford, patrons of the church in the Middle Ages. Some capable person(s) has produced a remarkable book, beautifully illustrated in colour, depicting the detailed history of the building. It is a real work of art. The miracle is that it remains on the bench without being securely padlocked to the wall.

Alongside the church is the Weare Gifford Hall a 15th century Manor House which still looks in prime condition. The small area around the church and manor House is just off the road through the village yet conveys an air of peace and quiet, which the traveller may enjoy, sat in a well-sited bench in the churchyard.

That is more or less the end of the walk. All that remains is to negotiate the last bit of the string bean to the car park. Although the walk ends here (for those who have used the Recreation Ground Car park) it is by no means the end of Weare Gifford - that is still some way off! Anyone wishing to partake of the amenities obtainable at the Cyder Presse will need to walk (or drive) or keep going a little longer.

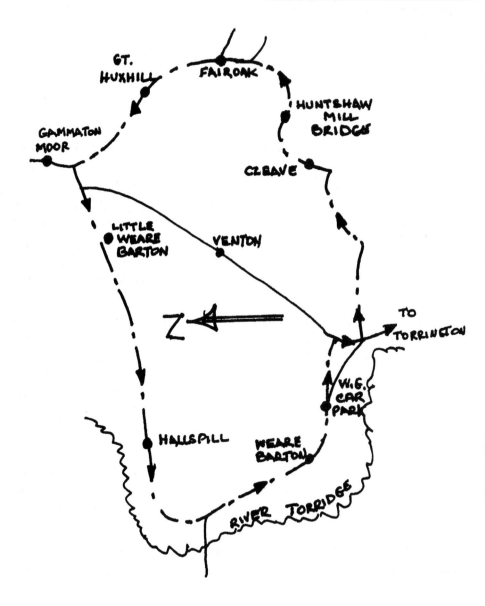

WALK 9

Weare Gifford —Cleave — Huntshaw Mill Bridge — Fairoak — Gammaton Moor — Hallspill — Weare Gifford.

7 Miles. *Map — OS Explorer 126 or139.*

Park as for walk 8 in the Parish car park (GR 470 222) or by arrangement with the landlord of the "Cyder Presse" (GR 478 220)

As before, from the Parish car park, cross the road at the east end and take the rather pleasant track which rises quite high above the road to allow some good views of the village. At the end of the track where it meets the narrow lane turn right to go down the hill.

Turn left at the FP sign by the thatched cottage and go up the "steps" in the far left-hand corner of the "garden". Cross over the stile and drop down to the corner of the field and then turn left to follow the line of the stream. There are two FP signposts to indicate these directions but age and weathering have caused them to blend in with the growth around.

The stream meanders in a deep tree-lined gully gently upwards to Southcott Barton. Where the stream goes into a culvert cross the field and the farm access road via a small gateway. Climb some more (or less) steps into a field which can be very messy underfoot. Keep to the left, again beside the route of the stream and pass the group of buildings at Southcott Barton.

There is aa slight problem at this point. The OS map clearly shows a public right of way beside a hedge or fence line across to the lane above Cleave. Indeed there is a FP sign and a stile in the side of the lane exactly where the footpath should be but all indications of any hedge/fence or footpath have been obliterated and the route now crosses an arable field. Rather than 'plough' across the field it is probably better to keep going by the stream and climb over the low dry stonewall on to the lane. Whichever route you choose turn right down the hill to Cleave.

Pass the "Granary" and "Barleycorn" and turn up left on to the lane signed for Huntshaw Mill and past Cleave farm. Carry on down the hill leaving the lowing of many cattle and the smell of silage behind to enjoy an excellent rural walk.

At Poolsteps the road drops very steeply to Huntshaw Mill Bridge. On reaching the T junction turn right to cross the bridge and almost immediately left on to the road signed for Huntshaw. In accordance with

Poolsteps

ancient custom, having crossed a river there is a hill to climb on the other side - this time quite steeply past Mill Cottage. The road bears round to the left with a pinewood on the right and a rather attractive man-made lake, complete with an island refuge in the middle, on the left.

The lane ends at Fairoak where it joins a slightly "mainer" lane. Turn left here to take the road to Gammaton moor and Bideford. Cross the bridge back over the river crossed earlier and up the hill with some wild woodland (happily no conifers this time) on the right.

Pass under the wires of one of the National Grid powerlines which are a feature of the area and which becomes a familiar sight on this walk. These great overhead power lines are of course absolutely vital to our well-being nowadays but it is a pity they cannot be made invisible! However, one should not be too critical. The thought of the countryside becoming infested with wind farms and mobile phone masts is infinitely worse.

Soon after the impressive Great Huxhill reach a T junction and turn right, shortly afterwards going under a second N G Powerline. At the 3 way cross take the turning on the left signed for Weare Gifford (and to the "Cheese Store"). Not far along bear off right to follow the lane to Hallspill (leaving customers for the cheese store to turn off). The road is inclined to

Huntshall Mill Bridge

be confined between high hedges in places but it is very high relative to the surrounding area thus offering tremendous all-round views where the hedges do not interfere. Ahead lies the great expanse of the River Torridge Valley and if visibility is good the dark shapes of Dartmoor Tors can be seen to the south-east. As one might expect in so exposed an area the winds from all quarters can be quite a feature as well.

The drop to Netherdown and Hallspill is quite steep but levels out as the road nears the river. A roadside sign warns of the danger of falling rocks at one point so mind your head although judging by the age and condition of the trees in the area there is probably more to fear from falling branches. Once safely past these hazards enter Weare Gifford and begin the long level trek along the elongated string bean of a village.

On the way pass a number of warning signs — "Road liable to flood" which should cause no concern unless there has been a Niagra of a deluge in your absence in which case you could be marooned for a while. Comfort may be derived in these circumstances from the thought that "The Cyder Presse" is no more than a mile's swim ahead. Under all normal circumstances the walk should end uneventfully at the Parish Car Park not far along the road.

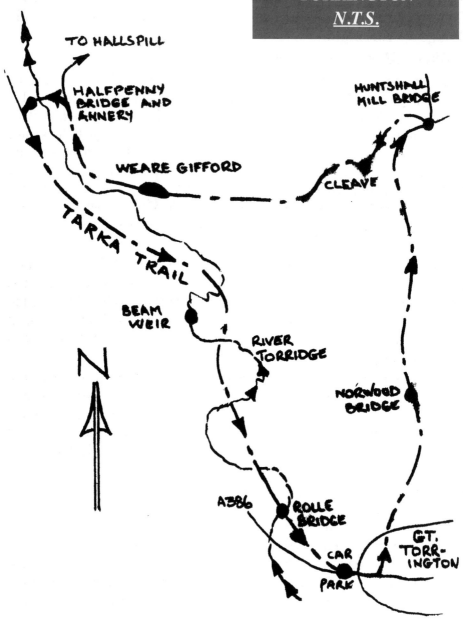

TO HALLSPILL

HALFPENNY
BRIDGE AND
ANNERY

HUNTSHALL
MILL BRIDGE

WEARE GIFFORD

CLEAVE

TARKA TRAIL

BEAM
WEIR

RIVER
TORRIDGE

N

NORWOOD
BRIDGE

A386

ROLLE
BRIDGE

CAR
PARK

GT.
TORR-
INGTON

WALK 10

Torrington Car Park on A386 (GR485194) — Dartington Glass Factory — Norwood Bridge — Huntshaw Mill Bridge — Weare Gifford — Halfpenny Bridge — Tarka Trail (South) — Rolle Bridge — Torrington.

9 Miles. *Map — OS Explorer 126.*

Anyone new to the area would do well to allow for an hour or two to be spent enjoying the historic town of Torrington. The car park is on the edge of town but within a short walking distance of the centre. It is a small place with narrow streets and a busy bustling shopping area in which the visitor is spoilt for choice where food and drink are concerned. The town proudly describes itself as the "Cavalier Town" in memory of the decisive battle in 1646 fought here during the Civil War. The Church of St. Michael stands high above the town and is a landmark for miles around but in February 1646 it blew up during the battle with disastrous consequences for the 200 Royalist prisoners incarcerated there.

The walk begins by leaving the car in the "Hot Dog" car park with a short walk along the pavement towards the town centre, past the cemetery. At the far end of the cemetery turn down left beside the wall and bear round to the right along the track. At the FP sign turn off right to follow the rough track with the back of town properties on one side and some fine views down the valley across Torrington Common.

Keep to this track with a factory building immediately ahead. This is in fact the Dartington Glass Factory, which is an interesting place to visit, and to take advantage of one of the conducted tours provided for visitors. Whether visitors shod in walking clodhoppers would be made welcome is not known. The external view of the buildings on approach is not exactly prepossessing, however although it may not be a pretty sight it is certainly economically important to the Town's economy.

At the end of the track where it goes right to the main road turn into the factory site where there is a yellow waymark arrow on a post. The public footpath runs through the loading area and into the extensive car parks. On reaching the far end of the building look for the FP sign just across the tarmac road. Not far down from the signpost opposite the gateway to the LP gas compound turn right to take the grass pathway through an area of scrubland.

Clamber over the stile, which leads down over the field, and leap over or crawl under (according to taste) the bar, which faces you at the bottom. Having crossed the bar, as it were, a short bit of tacky path leads to a cross-roads. Take the second road on the left, signed for Huntshaw and Gammaton (also Furze Farm), cross the stone bridge across the stream and enjoy a pleasant walk along a quiet country lane for a couple of miles. Drop down to a lovely spot at Norwood Bridge, up the hill to pass Furze Farm and then after a minor dip all the way down to the bridge at Huntshaw Mill and cross over it.

Norwood Bridge

At this point turn left where walkers who have completed Walk 9 will realize just what lies ahead. Those who haven't should prepare for a seriously steep ascent past the attractive little group of properties at Poolsteps. Pausing to admire them will allow for a most welcome breather before carrying on up the hill. You will eventually arrive at Cleave Farm and there turn right to pass "Barleycorn" and "Granary".

A little way up the lane you come across a stile and a FP sign on the left. The public footpath is routed across the field to Southcott Barton along the line of what (according to the OS Map) was once a hedge or fence but now open, arable land. If the field is under cultivation with no path provided it is preferable to continue further up the lane to the top of the field. There is a low stonewall to hop over and then a walk close to the hedge which bounds the stream.

At the entrance road to Southcott Barton go down over some DIY steps and cross the road to the small gate opposite. From this point follow the hedge and stream on the left all the way along until you reach the outskirts of Weare Gifford. A short way up the hill to the right on reaching the hedge at the end there is a stile (with an old FP sign) into the rear of a cottage on the left-hand side. Go down the "steps" into the garden area and out on to the road by the thatched cottage.

Turn right along the narrow road as far as the FP sign on the left which is the start of an excellent walk through a tree-lined area. At a Y junction take the lower track to emerge on to the road opposite the village hall car park in Weare Gifford. Keep straight on through the village for over half a mile unless you wish to make the slight diversion to have a look at what was the centre of the old village with its fine old church (see walk 8 for details) and old Manor House.

Towards the end of the village turn left to cross the Halfpenny Bridge (no toll payable now) to the ruins of the massive Annery Kiln, an old lime kiln with the appearance more of an ancient fortress. Continue on through Annery to go under the old railway line (now the Tarka Trail) and turn right along the side of the A386 for a few yards before turning into the Tarka Trail through a gateway. Again turn right. For the first mile or so the trail is below the A386 beside a high retaining wall. The other side is quite close to the R. Torridge with plenty of trees, which allow occasional glimpses of Weare Gifford on the opposite side, particularly in winter.

The track first takes a wide sweep round to the left to follow the course of the river and then an equally wide one to the right all of which makes for some interesting walking. However, the best is yet to come.

In rather less than a mile there are no less than three high and long bridges spanning bends in the river. The design and construction of this section of the railway was an impressive engineering undertaking, which must have cost an enormous amount of money at the time, money, which was probably never recouped in the life of the railway itself. But they built well which allows us today some of the finest walking imaginable. The views from these bridges are breathtaking set as they are in some lovely

Weare Gifford

wooded countryside.

We leave (possibly with a fringe of regret) the Tarka Trail at "The Puffing Billy" alias Torrington Railway Station. Any feelings of regret can be suitably assuaged by partaking of the comforts in the way of refreshments (which includes Real Ales) on offer in the old station building.

To continue on the final leg of the journey leave the station yard and turn left to cross Rolle Bridge. Just past the property "Corrie Fee" turn off the pavement and take the Alexander Path (it is signed).

The path is tarmac all the way up the hill and is a super walk through Torrington Common. It overlooks the steep valley down to your left and goes through some wide-open spaces, which provide a wonderful area for local townspeople to relax in a delightful, peaceful environment. The Alexander Path makes a most enjoyable end to a splendid walk.

Where the path ends at the top the car park lies to the right and while the walk ends there it really is worthwhile to remain long enough to look round Torrington as mentioned at the beginning of the walk.

Torrington Common

Torrington

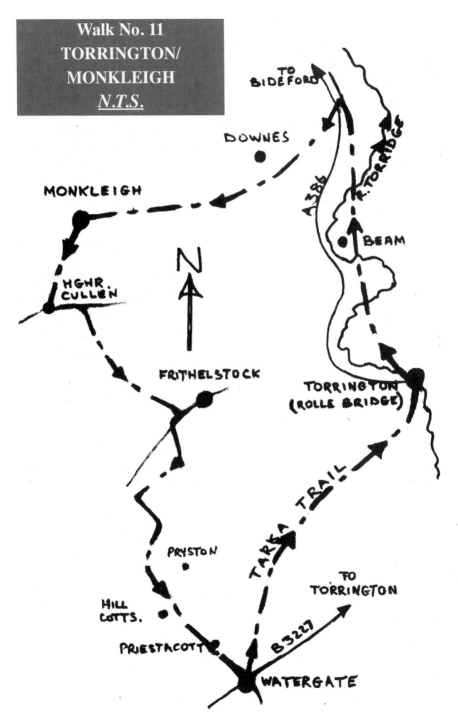

Walk No. 11
TORRINGTON/
MONKLEIGH
N.T.S.

TO BIDEFORD

DOWNES

MONKLEIGH

A386

R. TORRIDGE

BEAM

HGHR. CULLEN

N

FRITHELSTOCK

TORRINGTON
(ROLLE BRIDGE)

TARKA TRAIL

PRYSTON

HILL COTTS.

TO TORRINGTON

PRIESTACOTT

B3227

WATERGATE

WALK 11

Torrington — (RollE Bridge-A386) — Tarka Trail (North) — Monkleigh — Frithelstock — Watergate — Tarka Trail (North) — Torrington.

7 Miles. *Map — OS Explorer 126.*

Gaiters should be carried in case muddy conditions are to be expected. The best place to park is at the "Puffing Billy" at Rolle Bridge (GR480198). However, parking is severely limited and it may be necessary to use the public (free) car park at the top of the hill at GR 485195 particularly during holiday times in which case there is a short but steep walk down and back up the hill.

The walk as described will begin and end at the "Puffing Billy". Join the Tarka Trail at the back of the station and turn left towards Bideford. The path soon opens out into some lovely wooded country and in the distance of less than a mile there are three crossings of the River Torridge. Each of these is by high bridges giving spectacular views of the river and the surrounding countryside. The weir and bridge at Beam are particularly attractive and the keen photographer will be busy along this stretch.

After crossing the third of these bridges keep the eyes open for a subway on the left-hand side at Loxdown. This passes under the main A386 road where you leave the Tarka Trail and leads on to the narrow lane which winds gently uphill to Monkleigh village. It is a pleasant walk along a very quiet lane with woods on the left for half the way before giving way to more open countryside. Pass the entrance drive to Downes House and also the FP sign on the left and just keep going to Monkleigh.

On reaching the village turn left at the Primary School and through the churchyard of St. George's Church. The church will probably be locked but the well-kept graveyard has plenty to occupy anyone interested in local family names. One thing in particular which catches the eye is the War Memorial. It is a sobering thought to realize that a place as small as Monkleigh sent over 50 young men to serve in the 14/18 war of whom 7 did not return.

Turn right for a few yards after leaving the churchyard as far as the village hall where you turn left at the FP sign in the corner of the car park (walkers who have done Walk 7 will recognise it) and go down past the village hall itself. It is at this point when gaiters may become desirable on this walk. The route is down the roughish track, half-right to a gap in the hedge at the bottom of the field. The area is low-lying and can be quite messy at times.

Through the gap climb to the top right-hand corner of the field, go over the stile in the corner and keep going up beside the fence. This leads to a gateway (mind the barbed wire "wrapping" along the top rail of the gate) and from here strike diagonally across the field to another gateway situated close to a power pole. This gate leads on to a lane. A few yards along to the left leave the tarmac and turn off to the right at the FP sign so as to drop down over the field.

On arrival at the gateway go through and continue down to the foot-bridge over the stream at the bottom. Having crossed the bridge you will be confronted by the historical remains of what was once a perfectly normal gateway but now worthy of preservation as an ancient monument. Find a way through/over/round this bit of antiquity and walk along the more up-to-date line of duckboards to begin the rather steep climb up the field beside the hedge.

Clamber over the stile at the top and keep going. The area is quite high relative to the surrounding countryside and provides some extensive views from Monkleigh (behind you) round and across a great stretch of the River

Frithelstock

70

Torridge valley to your left. Come to a gateway (beware of a possible barbed wire barrier to duck under or climb over) before completing the short, final stage of the footpath where it meets the road close to the village of Frithelstock. The village is only a few yards off the route and is worth a short detour to admire this small, compact and historical settlement.

Our way is to the right but only as far as Six Acre Cottage where we turn off left at the FP sign into more fields. The bit to the top of the hill could be a little tricky so it is important to watch the navigation here. It is a case of bearing right, going round the hill rather than over the top of it. Look for two openings in the hedge and cross the stile in the right-hand gap. Turn immediately right to follow the hedge up to the field corner and round to the left to a gateway at the bottom. Once through the gate carry on down beside the bank which looks to have been a hedge at one time and go through the gate at the bottom of the valley.

Bear left up the track as far as the signpost and there turn sharply right along the top side of the fence. At the corner just follow the hedge all the way to the top and then left for a short distance to come out to the narrow lane near Hill Cottages.

Turn right and at Hill Cottages take the track on the left. Bear left to go round the topside of the somewhat sad farm at Priestacott which has clearly seen better days and just after the second gate take to the fields again by the FP sign.

Keep to the hedge as far as it goes and in the gap at the bottom carry on along the top of a bank, which is on the same line as the fence, has been. This leads to a rough tree-lined track down to meet the road at Watergate.

A few yards along the road to the left turn in to the Tarka Trail, again left, to begin the trek back to Torrington through some quite stunning woodland country with a stream on the left. It must have been a truly wonderful journey in the pre-Beeching days of railways. In many ways this is a great pity but the redeeming feature is that we now have a glorious track to walk along. Cyclists no doubt appreciate it as well. They would all be most welcome to walkers if only they had bells on their machines!

On the seats thoughtfully provided by the authorities, a wood-sculptor has been busily at work. First of all we meet a solitary, forlorn looking man sat comfortably contemplating the infinite, then a family group of Mum, Dad and progeny cosily cuddled up together. A third seat is occupied by a couple who seem to represent marital discord since they are sat at opposite ends of the seat. However, they at least have left enough room between them for a more loving couple to sit.

Rolle Bridge, Torrington

The end of the walk is nigh when you cross a long, high bridge across the valley and the River Torridge and again with some absolutely glorious views including the fine arched bridge at Rolle. So ends an excellent walk at the Puffing Billy where yet more delights await the connoisseur of real ales and big eats.

Quiet flows the River Torridge

Drummet's Mill

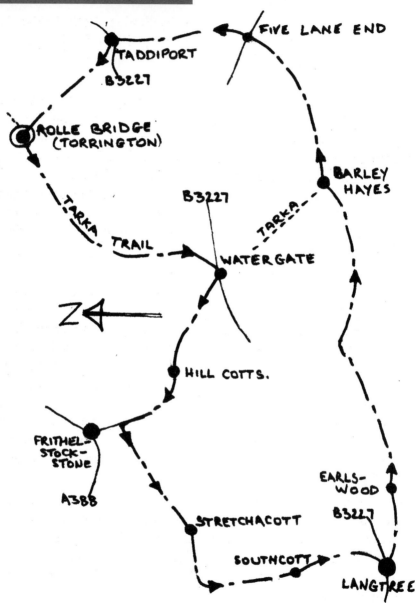

FIVE LANE END

TADDIPORT

B3227

ROLLE BRIDGE
(TORRINGTON)

BARLEY
HAYES

B3227

TARKA
TRAIL

TARKA

WATERGATE

Z

HILL COTTS.

FRITHEL-
STOCK-
STONE

A388

EARLS-
WOOD

STRETCHACOTT

B3227

SOUTHCOTT

LANGTREE

74

WALK 12
Torrington (Rolle Bridge) Car Park (GR480198) — Watergate — Priestacott — Frithelstockstone — Stretchacott — Langtree — Barley Hayes — Taddiport — Rolle Bridge.
10½ Miles. Map – OS Explorer 126.

Park at the car at the Torrington Railway Station, Rolle Bridge (now known by the more august title of "The Puffing Billy"). Begin walking by taking the Tarka Trail, south, down to Watergate. This is the section walked in Walk 11 only in the opposite direction this time.

Past Drummet's Mill and Mount Pleasant, through Pencleave Woods it is a superb walk beside a stream where you may be lucky enough to spot a heron gracefully gliding about its business of finding a tasty fish meal. In early spring the stream valley is a mass of wild daffodils, wild garlic and various marsh plants, which against the background of dense woodland are a joy to see. It is along this part of the Tarka Trail that the wood sculptor has been at work as mentioned in the previous walk where three of the bench seats provided for the benefit of walkers are occupied by life-like human figures. Apart from the one seat with a family apparently estranged they looked quite relaxed and peaceful.

The first part of the walk ends at the remains of an old platform at Watetgate where we leave the Tarka Trail to turn right up the road for a short distance before turning off right again by the public footpath sign (do not go through the wooden field gates adjoining the Tarka Trail). The track begins with an uphill climb through the woods and just past the last of the trees carry on through the gap in the hedge. Make for Priestacott Farm along the sunken track way. If the encroaching brambles present too much of an obstacle keep to the field edge instead. Where the track ends at a post with FP signs bear right for the gateway in the field above. Carry on up beside the hedge with Priestacott Farm on the left to the gateway leading on to the farm track.

Pause at this gateway to take a look behind and enjoy the extensive views across the valley before turning left to pass the ruins of what was once no doubt a typical old farm in better days. Follow the farm track out to the narrow road at Hill Cottages and turn left. Keep on this road as far as the T junction not too far ahead and there turn right for just under half a mile along another narrow road.

On reaching Hele lane Cottage you will find a small group of buildings with a track (signed) going off in front of the first building. Immediately opposite on the left-hand side of the road there is a stile neatly stashed away in a narrow gap in the hedge and this is the path to take. There is a FP sign but it could easily be missed if your attention wanders. However, all is not lost. By going straight on you will have the opportunity to pay a visit to Frithelstockstone although there is nothing really to see there. In this event turn about but this time look for a footpath on your right-hand side!

Keep to the side of the hedge right down into the valley and cross a stile and then a footbridge over the stream. From the stream, as one might expect, it is a case of going up this time through a fairly short length of track which can be marshy underfoot and infested with brambles and nettles which assail your person. Along this bit it is advisable to have gaiters and possibly a walking stick readily to hand. The ordeal is soon left astern and it is straightforward walking beside the hedge to the top of the hill.

A gateway at the top leads on to a concrete farm track and after passing a developing farm refuse dump you arrive at Stretchacott Farm where the public right of way passes through the middle of a large group of farm buildings. The drive leads eventually to the county road at which point turn left and look forward to about a mile and a half of quiet road walking into Langtree.

The character of the landscape changes to very open countryside, which apart from the views allows you to decide quite accurately which way, the wind is coming from. The land in this area has something of a moor land look about it judging by the extensive patches of reed. Pass the semi-derelict Heiberdown Cottage and press on down the hill to Townsend Farm first of all and then through Southcott, an old settlement nestling in the valley with a rather more prosperous look than some of the farms in the area.

Stay on the road down to the bottom of the valley and at the T junction bear left and soon afterwards turn off right to take the track (signed as unsuitable for motor vehicles - quite correctly too) up the steep hill past Woodhouse at which point the surfaced section gives way to a very rough RUPP - like track. It is quite steep. Arrive after a bit of a struggle (and

Entering Langtree

possibly breathless) on to a real county road where a right turn soon brings you to the gates of Langtree and the welcoming sign of "The Green Dragon".

This walk does not actually go through the village although only a slight detour is involved for anyone who wishes to have a look round. We turn left beside the "Green Dragon" (or via, according to how your fancy takes you - assuming it is open). A little way down the hill the road passes All Saints Church making it convenient to drop in for a few minutes.

Not far along the road at the 30mph signs turn left on to the tarmac drive-way leading to a small group of properties. Go past the track, which leads off left, and continue a few yards to a gateway on the right, opposite a big house. Go through this gateway, beside the FP sign, but only for a few steps. At the gap in the hedge turn left to follow the hedge/fence line at the back of the properties. Cross a stile, a short length of rough track and through a gateway to resume the walk along a hedge line. While completing this not-too-difficult manoeuvre spare a few moments to admire the vast panoramic views extending across the valley of the River Torridge.

The hedge ends at a small metal gate. Go through into the field and across to the old stone barn with a corrugated iron roof. Go through the gate by the near corner and wend your way through an overgrown area by following the yellow way mark signs. You have entered some wild "injun" country.

Just a little way down the grass path there is a parting of the ways. Take the path on the right which leads down the hill to a stream. Turn left along the bank, crossing two stiles and following the arrow signs which skirt round the south side of a property shown on the map as Earlswood. This drops down through some woods to a track parallel with but higher up than the stream. It is very pleasant but liable to be very messy underfoot.

Normal service is resumed where the woodland expedition meets a proper metalled track which is in fact the drive of Earlswood. Turn right and on reaching the county road turn left for a very pleasant walk along the valley on a quiet country lane. Pass a T-junction where the road on the left goes into Langtree and look for a narrow track on the right-hand side with a sign confirming its unfitness for motors.

Turn off by the sign and take the track to the road not far away and having reached the road turn left for a few yards before another turn, this time along a RUPP on the right-hand side.

Pass an interesting alfresco incinerator site (or possibly sight) and at a junction of RUPPS turn right for a short distance before turning left on to yet another RUPP this time with the tower of Little Torrington Church on the skyline right ahead.

The track, which had been quite good up to this point detiorates as it nears the road at Barley Hayes but only for a short stretch. Bear left to go under the bridge, which carries the Tarka Trail across the road at a pictur-esque spot before beginning a steepish climb up to West Ford Farm.

The road leads up to Five Lane End where you cross straight over to join a narrow, quiet road bounded by Devon hedges. Take the left-hand fork at the top of the hill and begin the long descent into Taddiport. Take care on reaching the main B3227 road at Taddiport. Keep straight on down to the bridge over the River Torridge. This is the sort of place to stop and admire the river views which are really splendid but again take care because the road is busy and the bridge old and very narrow.

At the far end of the bridge turn off the road for over half a mile of

The weir and bridge at Taddiport

lovely riverside walking. No more roads or hills - just virtually level walking in delightful surroundings - at least once past the old milk factory on the right!

However, we can be grateful to the builders of the factory because they have left a legacy of a weir across the river. At least it would appear from the pumping station on the bank that the weir was constructed to ensure an adequate water supply for the factory. Whatever the reason it is a valuable asset. What is the eternal fascination of weirs, one wonders? Rivers in their natural state are attractive but somehow or other a weir adds another dimension. Salmon appreciate them too it would seem.

Some way along the path another interesting phenomenon is to be found. This one is not so beautiful as the weir but is an essential amenity for a civilized community and is not altogether unattractive. It is known as the sewage treatment works for Torrington and we leave it at that.

A little further on the low-lying area has been well-planted with poplars which create an idyllic setting beside the river. It is an ideal spot to sit relaxing for a few minutes possibly finishing off any food and drink left in the rucksack.

Rolle Bridges, Torrington

All that remains is to clamber up onto an elevated footpath where the riverside walks terminates and turn left to go under the bridge carrying the Tarka Trail over it. A few yards further on turn up right through a stone arch on to the Tarka Trail where a left turn soon brings you to the Puffing Billy and the conclusion of an eventful, satisfying day.